A Can of Words

Editors:
Heather Armstrong and Carol Green

A Can of Words

A collection of poems and drawings by young women who have been sexually abused.

Date of Publication:
1997

Published by:
Wedgewood Books
14 Hollins Close
Whitehaven
Cumbria
CA28 8EX

Printed by:
Small Print
The Malthouse
Llangollen
LL20 8HS
Tel: 01978 861990

Some of the contributors to this book have changed their names for legal reasons.

All proceeds from the sale of this book will go to the NSPCC

(Charity Registration Number: 216401)

A Can of Words

Editors:
Heather Armstrong and Carol Green

A Can of Words

Acknowledgements

We would like to thank Ashley Cooper for his invaluable assistance in enabling our ideas to become a reality and our colleagues at the Wedgewood Centre for their ongoing support.

We are indebted to the Prince's Trust for their generous financial backing and we would also like to thank Cumbria County Council, Copeland and Allerdale Area Committees and Copeland Borough Council and Northern Arts for their financial support.

We would also like to thank Paula Jackson, Keith Richardson and Michael Nixon for their help in reproducing the illustrations and the front cover.

Contents *Page*

Illustrations	*Page*

Introduction to the Editors

Heather Armstrong and Carol Green have worked at the Wedgewood Centre since it was established in West Cumbria in 1992. The Wedgewood Centre is a partnership between NCH Action for Children, NSPCC and Cumbria Social Services and was set up to provide long term therapeutic work for children who have suffered abuse and trauma, in particular sexual abuse.

Both Heather and Carol are qualified social workers and play therapists and have extensive experience of undertaking both individual and group work with children and young people who have been sexually abused.

Heather Armstrong is employed by NCH Action for Children. Carol Green is employed by the NSPCC.

Introduction to the Book

The idea for this book developed from our work at the Wedgewood Centre, and in particular our contact with the young people whose poems are included here.

Sexual abuse is still taboo. In publishing this book we want the strength and courage of these young people to be acknowledged and to enable them to have a voice to speak out and break the silence that makes it hard to tell and heal.

In compiling the book, we struggled with how best to acknowledge each young person's journey of recovery whilst also highlighting the broader therapeutic process and the important similarities in their feelings. We decided to focus on each individual's journey from victim to survivor highlighting their individual strengths and struggles. We feel that by doing this the book also reflects the similarities in their experience and feelings.

The emotions expressed throughout this book are intense, reflecting the depth of feeling that exists as a result of their experiences.

We hope that this book will act as an inspiration to other young people on their journeys to recovery and also to encourage those who have yet to start. Finally, we hope that it will help others become aware of the pain of sexual abuse.

Our thanks go to each of the contributors for trusting us with their work. We have been privileged to accompany them on their journey.

Carol and Heather

Angela

Hi, I'm Angela and I'm 17 years old. I've lived in Whitehaven for the past 9 years. I was born in Scotland. I live with my mum, brother Bob and sister Mary. I have another sister Tricia, she lives near us with her fiancé Gavin and her 1 year old son Gavin Jnr. My family are the most important people in my life.

When I was 6 years old my step-dad sexually and emotionally abused me and Tricia. What he did brought me and Trish closer but drove a wedge between me and Trish and the rest of the family. When Tricia was 16 she went to live in Scotland. I was angry at first, but then I realised that she went to keep herself sane. Living with him was cracking her up. When I was 13 he was arrested and is now half way through his sentence. In the 3 years without him we have become a real family again. We're all closer than we've ever been.

I wrote these poems to help get my head sorted, I am slowly coming to terms with the abuse, with help from Heather and the support from my family. Thanks.

If reading our book helps one person to break the silence then it's worth all the hard work it took putting it together.

Thanks for making it possible Heather and Carol.

Love Ang.

My Life

love
rape
My Life!!
good
Pleasures
CRIME
child's play
Mind and body
power
sex
love
AGONY
REVENGE
dirty
help
teenager's
Family
FREE
tell
Talk
therapy
got a co
TEMPER
safe
STRONG

Silence

When I was 10 years old
I knew what rape was
And murder too.

'Cos I'd see them regularly
On the news.

But although it was happening to me
I'd never heard of sexual abuse.

I understand that it's taboo
But it shouldn't be
You see it just made it harder for me
I'd never seen it on the news
Or been told that it was wrong
I thought it was normal
So I suffered on.

My Body

Your hands touch and caress,
Your fingers knead and press,
Bottom, legs and breast,
I am your daughter,
But you don't care,
You see a body lying there.

Your hands all over,
How can you do this,
How can this be real?

Numb

An $^{1}/_{8}$ of pot, a wrap of speed,
A few hours of bliss is all I need.
Bottle of cider, couple of cans,
Now I can't feel his hands.
A couple of trips, I have no fear,
Can't even smell him
Now he's near.

My Life

Did you get a buzz
From seeing me scared.

Did you enjoy
Me submitting through fear.

Did the sight
Of a child's naked body
Stir you inside.

Or did you just enjoy
Having control of my life.

Web

So far my life has been
A huge web of
Lies, secrets and deceit.

I deceived everyone
By lying for him
And keeping it all a secret.

I was like a spider
Living in a web
But my web wasn't made of silken threads
But lies, secrets and deceit.

My Monster

There was a monster in my room, when I was a little girl
He lurked in corners 'til I was alone
Then he came out to play
But we never played chase or dolls
His games were secret and frightened me
But I said I'd never tell.

There was a monster in my room, when I was a little girl
He lurked in corners 'til I was alone
Then he came out to play
But we never played cars or trains
We played his secret game,
Called touch and feel
He said if I ever told
They would take me away
So I kept quiet and played.

He would touch and feel
I would plead and squeal
But my monster stayed.

I always knew one day I'd tell
Now my monster can rot in hell.

Bullshit

'I do it because I love you',
Is what you always said.

'You know I really care for you',
As you lead me to your bed.

'I know you enjoy it',
As you remove my clothes.

'Don't tell your mum',
As you pull me close.

'She wouldn't understand',
As you touched with your hand.

Why you told me all this bullshit,
I'll never understand.

Sorry

You've admitted it
You took the blame
You've got all the shame
So why am I not happy.

You're taking your punishment
You're living with the guilt
You're out of our lives for good
So why am I not happy.

You've said, 'I did it'
You've said 'It was my fault'
But there's one thing you forgot
And it's the most important one of all.

You've never said, 'I'm sorry'.

Trust

I can't trust anyone
I'm afraid they'll hurt me.

I can't trust anyone
They always disappoint me.

I can't trust anyone
Because you've nearly destroyed me.

The only person I can truly trust
Is me.

And that's because of you.

The Child

The child is gone
Lost forever.

She was innocent
You were cruel.

She trusted you and needed you
But you were not there
It was your love that killed her.

She needed a father
But you were not there.

She needed love
But got perversion
You forced her into submission
And killed her.

The child is gone, lost forever.

Tricia

We were together
As two we were strong
But then one day
You were gone.

I was sad
And ashamed now
To admit I was mad.

Sad because you left me
With him on my own.

I can see now
My anger was wrong.

I'm grateful to you
Because you were strong.

Strong enough for both of us
And now he's gone.

So Tricia,
I'd like to say thank you
And let you know, I think
You're the greatest person I know.

I Love You.

Mum

I'm sorry I lied and kept it from you.

I never thought you'd understand
But you did
I thought you'd hate
But I was wrong.

Thank you for keeping me strong.

Changed

I was weak and subdued
I was scared and removed
You made me that way
And you thought that's how I'd stay.

I've changed
I'm stronger, tougher and no longer scared
Because I've discovered how many people care.

Changed

Leanne

I was sexually abused by my father for a long, long time. I remember the last year specifically but the rest of it is just flashbacks. We started as a perfect family you know, he was the ideal dad, top job, he always played with the neighbourhood kids, the dad everyone wanted, well that's what they thought. It was always like that at least on the outside. On the inside, the inside that only I saw, he was evil. He had a major drink problem (not even my mum knew) but he was my dad and yes I still loved him. That's why I never told a soul. He was one great big lie.

I told when I was 12 or 13. My poems were the only way I could open up. It was like my escape release. I have a younger brother, 3 years younger but my dad never touched him, thank God. I felt sometimes as if it was all just in my head, you know, as if I'd imagined it because my dad denied it and said I was mentally ill. He got away with it and of course a lot of people believed him. My pen and paper were my friends they made it more real, I wasn't crazy.

I would like my poems published because I hope that someone out there can look at them and say yeah, I know what you mean. Plus I thought people who got abused only came from bad or broken homes but mine was ideal, too good. I don't want anyone else to think this. I'd like to take this opportunity to thank my mam who stood by me and all my shit, even after being married to him for over 20 years. She believed me. Also my fiancé who put me back on the tracks, thank you and I love you both. Now I'm happy and I live with my boyfriend and I am expecting a child of my own. I'm only 17 but my baby is no mistake. I'm just more mature than most people because of what happened, I grew up fast. I'll never forget but I can get on with my life and believe me one day you'll feel the same and put it behind you the way I have. I have a future and a baby to look to now.

There is light at the end.

Be a Daddy

You made promises
You never kept

From you all I wanted
Was arms outstretched

A kiss and love
Like a child should get

But all I got was sex and threats.

?

Why do I always feel so down?

Why do I have a permanent frown?

Why have I got bags under my eyes?

I'll tell you why,
Coz he told lies.

He should be punished,
For what he's done.

Why did he do it?
Did he think it was fun?

Anger and Frustration

Getting dark around me
I'm clinging to the floor
Hiding in a corner
He's coming through the door.

Slowly comes towards me
Please give me some light
But black is all I see
Let me put up a fight.

Nothing here is said
I'm alive but I feel dead
I'm scared I'm gonna fall.

He's gone,
That's it,
That's all.

Depression

Why does this feeling
Come to me.

Why won't it go,
Let me be free.

Stress, shakes, tears,
Stupid bloody fears.

Why won't it go away,
Let me smile,
For a day.

The Dark

Why is it there?
What have I done?
If I tell you what,
You'll laugh and make fun.

Why is it there?
Why is it cold?
Why am I scared?
I'm sixteen years old.

I thought only kids were scared of this,
I wish it was possible to give it a miss,
But it comes around every night,
And takes away all the light.

A Poem to my Childhood

Don't cry little one,
You broke free,
And now he's gone.

Even through the times,
You thought you'd die,
You kept strong,
Your head was high.

Please don't be sad,
Please don't cry,
He did bad
He did lie.

To Him, Dad, Abuser, Dickhead

You were the one who abused me,
Then had the nerve to accuse me.

I lived with that,
And couldn't feel free,
Of all the guilt,
That you gave me.

But that was the child,
That you have killed,
And all the gaps
I now have filled.

You do sometimes,
Break the seal,
But not for long,
Coz I can heal.

Louise

I am Louise and I am 17. When I was 13 I was raped by two male strangers. I kept this to myself for two years during which I became anorexic, felt dirty, guilty, useless and humiliated. I am now aware that it wasn't my fault and that I'm not the only one. I can now deal with my feelings in better ways thanks to a very understanding boyfriend and have worked hard to rebuild my life. It's taken a while but it was worth it.

I wrote this poem to express how I feel now and to remind myself how far I have come.

I wanted my poem to be published to help others who have been in similar situations and to let them know it gets better, and to help me to deal with it.

Monsters

These are my monsters all messed up.

I am sitting on the top as a child and a teenager because I defeated the monsters who messed me up. It took a long time and was a hard struggle to reach the top, but now every time I walk I trample on them. Now I am looking away from them and to a good future.

Keep climbing!

Then and Now

It, what happened has passed,
The memory is still there.

The consequences, my actions have passed,
The scars are still there.

The guilt, the confusion has passed.
My feelings are still there.

The past has finally passed,
And my future is finally there.

Rachel

I was sexually abused by my uncle from when I was 6 until I was 15 years old. It stopped when I found the courage to tell a teacher. Nothing happened to him.

I started to write poems as I did not feel there was anybody I could talk to and I still had a lot more to say. I found writing things down quite safe. When I disclosed everything to Carol I started to share some of my earlier poems. However, I still felt that it was safer to write some things down rather than say them.

When I joined the Brave Tellers*, I realised that I wasn't alone. After all the help I've had from Wedgewood I now know I'm not a victim but a survivor. I would like my poems published so that others know that they are not alone and that they too can be survivors instead of victims.

*The Brave Tellers was the Older Girls Group which ran from March 95 to July 95. (Tellers was an anagram of the first initials of our first names and Brave is what we all are). For me personally, it was the first time I had realised that I wasn't alone in how I felt. During the 5 months of the group, we all shared an awful lot of feelings and experiences; this needed a lot of trust, respect and friendship. We were all able to offer each other support and know that we would be supported back.

It's Happening Now

Said father to daughter, listen to what I say
These are my rules which you have to obey
I have the right to make you my special girl
I am allowed to make you the centre of my world
What we have is secret, only we know
If mum knew she'd be upset, she'd blame you and go

So daughter listens to daddy
Like all little girls should do
Tries to tell herself he doesn't mean all the pain
He puts her through
She knows he's an adult
Aren't adults always right?
But she still doesn't like what he does to her at night

Said uncle to niece, this is our game
The one you like to play
It's all your fault it's happening today
But don't tell your cousin, your aunt or your friend
Or I'll make sure this never ends

So niece listens to uncle
Like all little girls do
But she doesn't like him hurting her
She doesn't like what he makes her do

Said boy to girl, you don't really mean no
Just let this happen - then you can go
This is why you came to see me
You only want one thing
This'll be fun - it's not pain it brings

(continued)

So girl listens to boy, she hasn't a choice
She's tried to say no but he doesn't hear her voice
She tries to block it out, forget he's there
Whatever she does, he doesn't care

Said mother to son, don't be afraid
It's happening to lots of boys today
This is normal, it makes us friends
But don't tell your dad or the family will end

So son listens to mum
Like all boys do
He tries to tell himself
She doesn't mean the pain she puts him through

One day maybe they'll all decide they've had enough
If the secrets are so special
Why are the nights so tough?
Do they have to put up with it
Pain, hurt and fear
I know the answer - that's why I'm here
But for all the people living with it
The answer won't be clear

He Just Went Ahead

She said No but he didn't care
He just went ahead and raped her
Then and there
He didn't stop for one second to think
Of the misery he'd cause
He just went ahead and raped her
Then walked right out of her door

And when she went to fight him
To put him where he belonged
He lied and told a story
Convinced them she was wrong

What could she do?

She'd been raped then let down
Humiliated twice
Had to tell her story
Had to tell the worst part of her life
Each time she told more
The pain stabbed her like a knife
He'd made her tell her story
He'd damaged the rest of her life.

I

I sometimes wish I was dead
There's no sense running through
There's no help in a particular way
I'm stopped from hating you
I don't know why it's my fault
Maybe it's something I did
I don't understand your reasons
You stopped me being a kid

It's

It's a really weird feeling
Confused, down and stressed
Some say you need loving
Others - tablets 'you're depressed'
But no one tells me where help is
Just expect me to carry on and smile
But I'm not a 10 minute job
This could take a while.

Masks

This is my mask, it's not the real me
It means what you get
Isn't always what you see
I have many different masks
To hide each way I feel
Maybe soon I'll not have to wear a mask
And I'll wear a face that's real

Life

Two steps forward, three steps back
Cider, beer, an 'E', some crack
Substances to numb the pain
Believing then that you are sane
Finding ways of keeping it in
Snorting, smoking, injecting it in
Ruining your body, not giving a damn
This is a life? What a complete sham.

Will You

If I believe in you - will you hurt me?
If I trust in you - will you let me down?
If I share with you - will you stop me?
If I cry - will you laugh?
If I laugh - will you laugh with me?

If you believe in me - I won't hurt you
If you trust in me - I won't let you down
If you share with me - I won't stop you
If you cry - I won't laugh
If you laugh - I'll laugh with you
Not at you
Not now
Not ever
I believe in you
Believe in me?

Knots

A huge knot inside of your stomach
All twisted and pulled tight
All loose ends have been tied together
So no loose threads hang out.

An unhappy feeling
A feeling of hurt and pain
You want to pull it open
You want rid of the hurt and shame.

You never find any answers
Never manage to find out why
So you lock your feelings up
Become hard - no tears - you don't cry.

Little by little you pull apart the string
Loosen a few knots
Become able to share your 'story'
Try and understand things.

Anger

Anger is the clash of fear, hurt and rage
It's a feeling of madness, emptiness and pain
Of telling yourself one thing and feeling another
Of hurting deep inside and layering on the covers

Fear of being scared, hurt or upset
Of having to face something which you'd rather forget

Hurt from an experience or something that's hard
So you brick up your wall and put up your guard

Rage of pain, being screwed up inside
Thinking that your feelings have died

Feelings can hurt, can tear you apart
Can mangle your head up and split up your heart

For Carol and Others

It's because I know I can trust you
It's because you give a damn
That I can share my thoughts with you
And know you'll try to understand

It's because you don't laugh at me
Or tell me that I'm wrong
It's because you give me confidence
And help me believe I'm strong

It's because I know you'll be there
To talk to, or maybe to cry
It's because I know you really do care
That's what makes me try

Rainbow

When things go wrong, as they sometimes will,
When you don't think you can climb your hill.
Stop the bad thoughts, think for a while.
Put your frown away and give a big smile.

The Brave Tellers

We started off as the Girls Group
Then we got a name
We were called the Brave Tellers
Thursday nights were never the same.

Going through our feelings
Sorting out right from wrong
Wrestling with strange emotions
Trying to smile as we went along.

At times I think we hated you both
For what you were asking us to do
At times it felt like you were trying
To open our minds
We weren't sure if we could let you through.

So now we've come to the finish
The group's time has come to an end
And the saddest thing for me
Is that I'll miss my new friends.

o o o

Remember when we first started
The scaredness and the fear
Then we got to know each other better
We weren't afraid to show our tears
We shared an awful lot of ourselves
During our months together
But we always knew, no matter how bad
We had each other, Carol and Heather!

The Brave Tellers

2nd March to 20th July 1995

Trisha

Hi, I'm Trisha, I'm 21 and I have a one year old son, who is the most important person in my life along with his father. I am very close to my family but we did not always get along so well. Over the past three years there's been a stronger bond between us all.

When I was about 6 or 7 my stepfather started to abuse me, not just sexually but emotionally as well. He did so without any guilt until I ran away when I was 16. He also abused my younger sister Angela for a long time. I hated myself for leaving Angela behind with him.

One year later I told my auntie about what he had done. They phoned the police and he was picked up and remanded in custody. Then a few months later he was sentenced to 6 years in prison. He has now done 3 years, he went for parole but was refused because he doesn't think that what he did was wrong, because we were not his real daughters (sad man). He thought it was like having an affair. He doesn't care what he's done to us. He'll never realise how much he hurt us and how betrayed we felt. He didn't deserve to be our stepfather. He doesn't deserve to be my sister Mary's father.

I felt sorry for Mary, he's her father. She was stuck in the middle, she loves us but she doesn't know how she feels about him. Whereas I know I hate him and will never forget or forgive him for what he has done to me, Angela and our family.

I wrote these poems because I was going through a hard time, I kept getting flashbacks of what he had done to me. Angela told me she had written some poems at Wedgewood and it helped her a lot. So I tried it, I was amazed how easy the words just appeared on the paper. Writing my poems helped me to move on and put my memories to the back of my head. They'll never go but they've faded.

I would like my poems to be published to show Bobby that I'm not ashamed any more and I've picked up the pieces of my shattered life and I've survived. Maybe he'll understand that what he did was wrong - maybe he'll even feel ashamed of what he's done. I hope the book will help children who are being abused or have been, to take back control of their lives and become a survivor not a victim.

Stop

You didn't hear
Or see the fear
All you did was pull me near
I had no hands
No hands to make you stop

I heard the words in my head
But they were never said
Please stop, I want you to stop
They were hard to say
Would you have stopped anyway

Stop
It's not a long word
So easy to say
So please stay the fuck away

I hurt so much
'Cos I wanted to say
The words that would make you stay away

The Touching Game

A look, a touch
You wanted too much
You thought it was a game
You touched till you came

Come I'll show you the touching game
You make me sick
You're such a prick
My world's in a spin
'Cos you wanted to win

You were in my dreams
No one heard my screams
The games we played
Were the ones you made

The memories you made
Will someday fade
You took everything I had
That's what makes me mad

The Days Before You

There was a child I knew
In the days before you
A happy child
Full of life
Then my mother became your wife

Things were good, at first
Then you changed
The protector became the attacker
That's when things got bad

My happy days had gone
The loving child
Turned to a hateful one
Who lied and hurt people
To make her feel better

The fun stopped then
The child had gone and
Left a bitter teenager
Full of hate

I wished you would go
I wished you dead
But you're still in my head

The days before you
Were good
I wished my mother wasn't your wife
But then Mary wouldn't be in our life

In the days before you
I used to smile
Those days have ended
They can never be mended

Dreams

My dreams were filled with you
My days were filled with pain
I had no escape
That's why it's called RAPE

You were like a shadow
Everywhere I turned
You were there
I could always feel your stare

I would wake from a dream
And hear my scream
Your face was there to greet me
That always freaked me

I would blush with embarrassment
I would tremble with fear
'Cos I knew you were near
I knew one day it would end
'Cos you were never a friend

Feelings

When I heard you climb the stairs
I tried to hide my fears
You wanted to look
You wanted to touch
You knew it made me mad
You knew it made me sad

You made me cry
You made me sigh
You knew it was wrong
But you still carried on

How scared I felt
'Cos I had no help
No one knew
'Cos people liked you

You hurt me bad
When I made you mad
Sad and scared
Is all I knew
MAN DO I HATE YOU

A Thousand Questions

There's a thousand questions
I'd like to ask
Where do I start
Why me? How? Why Angela?
There's three for a start

I thought it was something you saw in me
Something bad
Or something that made you mad
I wasn't the one to blame
You should have all the shame

We didn't deserve the life we had
All the pain, shame and sorrow
But now we have a tomorrow

What question next
Did you not feel any guilt?
'Cos you knew how we felt
How does it feel to know
The love we once felt
So easily turned to HATE

Guilt

The guilt I had
Made my heart sad
If only I could forget
There would be no regret

You were meant to be my father
But that didn't matter
You had the fun
I wished I had a gun

What was on my mind
Was the one thing I couldn't find
The guilt I felt
Made my heart melt

Closer, closer you would slide
How I felt the sickness inside
You were on my mind
That's why the sun never shined

The things I've seen
Should never have been
Now you've gone
I'm the one having fun

Angela

We have shared
All the sadness
And all the madness
But still I feel helpless

I look at you
And see the pain
I want to help
But what can I do?

Your sky will soon be blue
No more dark clouds for you
Nothing will hold you down
Once you find your way around

TAKE CARE OF YOU

Together

Together we are strong
Together we are one
Together we can keep him out of sight
We can keep up the fight

The past haunts us
The fear we feel
Is so unreal
He can't get us now
'Cos he's fenced all around

Still we live in fear
Of the day he's fenced no more
But we are strong
We can carry on

Together we can make it
Together we will stand

Tez

I was sexually abused by an adult male friend of the family when I was 13 years old. He denied the allegations and there was no prosecution.

I wrote these poems shortly after my 15th birthday when I was feeling down and found it a good way to express my feelings.

I want my poems published to help people who have (or haven't) spoken about their abuse, so they can see other people have these feelings and emotions, and to let them know they are not alone.

Thank you to everybody in the CFCC group, also to Heather and Carol who helped the most, without you it wouldn't have worked.

Betrayed

How could you betray my trust
When I trusted you with all my love
It was all just a joke for you
I hope you listen to the above

How dare you shout in the street
I'll try not to be beat
Oh how people would love to know
What lies under that image of yours

Please don't come near again
I just can't handle the pain
You'll never learn
Of all the things that churn
Inside someone's heart

Of all the stupid things I did
I trusted you
You're free to the highest bid
I need to be free of you
So I can learn to live again.

Helpful Names and Addresses

Childline: Freepost 1111 (No Stamp Needed)
LONDON
N1 0BR
Telephone: 0800 1111 (Free Phone)

Offers free advice and counselling to children.

NSPCC Child Protection Helpline:
See telephone directory for local branch of NSPCC
Telephone: 0800 800 500 (Free Phone)
0800 056 0566 (minicom)

Helpline offers 24 hour nationwide counselling and advice service.

National Drugs Helpline: Telephone: 0800 776600

Police: See local telephone directory or in an emergency,
Telephone: 999

Royal Scottish Society for the Prevention of Cruelty to Children:
Melville House
41 Polworth Terrace
EDINBURGH
EH11 1NU
Telephone: 0131 337 8539

Offers advice about child abuse.

Rape Crisis: Telephone: Carlisle 01228 36500
or see local telephone directory.

Samaritans: Telephone: 0345 909090 (at local rate)

Social Services Department:
See local telephone directory, listed under name of County or City.

The Wedgewood Centre:
14 Hollins Close
WHITEHAVEN
Cumbria
Telephone: 01946 693359

Support for children and their families who have been affected by sexual abuse.

Youth Enquiry Service: See local telephone directory.